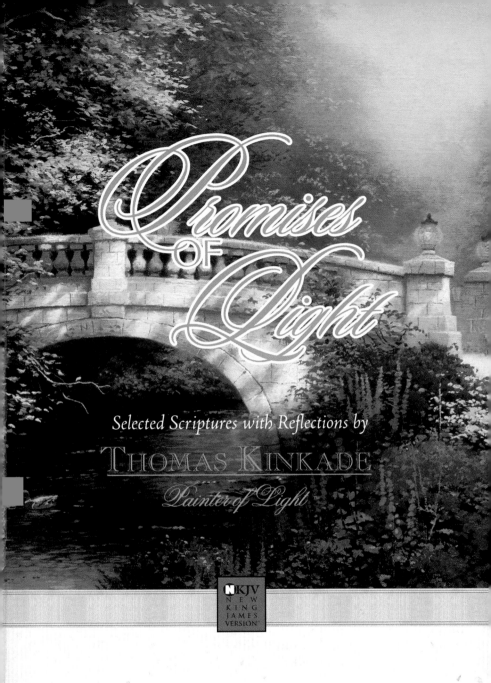

Promises
OF
Light

Selected Scriptures with Reflections by

THOMAS KINKADE
Painter of Light

NKJV
NEW
KING
JAMES
VERSION

THOMAS NELSON PUBLISHERS
Nashville

presented to

_____

from

_____

date

_____

3

Contents

5 | Gallery of Paintings

8 | Come Grow with Me

12 | Promises of Truth

32 | The Light of Salvation

52 | The Light of Hope

72 | Strength Renewed

92 | Celebrations of Praise

112 | Special Thoughts and Memories

Gallery of Paintings

Promises of Truth

The Bible—Our Comfort, Guide, and Strength

12-13 The Victorian Garden

16-17 Gardens Beyond Autumn Gate

20-21 Beyond Autumn Gate

24-25 Cobblestone Brooke

28-29 The Blessings of Spring

The Light of Salvation

Promises That God Saves from Sin

32-33 Spring Gate

36-37 Pools of Serenity

40-41 Blossom Bridge

44-45 Glory of Morning

48-49 Foxglove Cottage

Gallery [continued]

The Light of Hope
Promises for Spiritual Growth

52-53	Gardens Beyond Spring Gate
56-57	Rose Gate
60-61	Spring at Stonegate
64-65	The Garden of Prayer
68-69	Summer Gate

Strength Renewed
Promises for Your Personal Needs, Family and Relationships

72-73	The Open Gate
76-77	Cobblestone Village
80-81	Hollyhock House
84-85	Studio in the Garden
88-89	Home Is Where the Heart Is II

Gallery [continued]

Celebrations of Praise

*Promises of the Triumph of Righteousness,
and Psalms of Worship and Praise*

92-93	Hidden Cottage
96-97	Winsor Manor
100-101	Chandler's Cottage
104-105	Evening at Merritt's Cottage
108-109	Everett's Cottage

Come Grow with Me

I'm not the only one who thinks so. God knows—there's just something special about gardens. It was His earliest picture of perfection—the place where He once walked and fellowshipped with man face-to-face. Though I wasn't there at that beautiful beginning, I only have to wander into nature where I hear and see His heart in the quiet of His creation. And I rejoice because, in Christ, we still have that place of perfect peace with God.

That's why I love to plant gardens. Some of them you'll see in this book—only my canvas is the soil, my brush the hoe, and paint the wellspring of life that makes the picture thrive. As I work in my studio (or preferably on the deck behind my house), I can't help but think of the similar joy God must feel in cultivating for Himself a people destined to bloom and grow under His care. We, His children, are His garden of love—God's own masterpiece.

But I have not forgotten that this isn't Eden. As long as we live on this earth, we struggle under the searing heat of sin. We wrestle with the weeds that would choke out our faith. We chase away—again and again—the enemies that would devour the precious seed of hope Christ has sown in us. But do not be dismayed. God knows. And He has made provision. We have His promise.

Though we feel the threat of death, we fling ourselves fully on Christ, God's lifeline given in His Word. His Scripture nurtures our souls like the richest soil, and feeds us nutrients we need to grow in Him. Each promise of God to complete the work He has begun in us builds another strand of strength as our roots wrap ever deeper, ever tighter around His grace. The result? A beautiful creation of God, firmly rooted in truth so that the fragrant petals of faith and love can flourish in even the harshest environment.

So come grow with me as we dig deeply into God's garden of unfailing promises. And rejoice as our face-to-face fellowship with Him brings forth fruit in its season.

He shall be like a tree planted

by the rivers of water,

that brings forth its fruit in its season,

whose leaf also shall not wither;

and whatever he does shall prosper.

PSALM 1:3

Promises of Truth

The Bible—Our Comfort, Guide, and Strength

Without the ground, a garden cannot grow.
Neither can our souls without our spiritual bedrock—the Bible.
It is here, through the words of God Himself, that we encounter
Christ at life's very core. It is here where we surrender our souls
to His tender tools. Where He tills, waters, and wills us to grow
until our mustard-seed faith shoots forth branches that bear
His image and beckon others to come rest in His shade.

*A*ll Scripture is given by inspiration of God,

and is profitable for doctrine, for reproof,

for correction, for instruction in righteousness,

that the man of God may be complete,

thoroughly equipped for every good work.

2 TIMOTHY 3:16-17

"*H*eaven and earth will pass away,

but My words will by no means pass away."

MARK 13:31

For the word of God is living and powerful,

and sharper than any two-edged sword,

piercing even to the division of soul and spirit,

and of joints and marrow, and is a discerner

of the thoughts and intents of the heart.

HEBREWS 4:12

My son, do not forget my law,

but let your heart keep my commands;

for length of days and long life

and peace they will add to you.

PROVERBS 3:1-2

Every word of God is pure;

He is a shield

to those who put their trust in Him.

PROVERBS 30:5

"For as the rain comes down,
and the snow from heaven,
and do not return there,
but water the earth,
and make it bring forth and bud,
that it may give seed to the sower
and bread to the eater,
so shall My word be
that goes forth from My mouth;
it shall not return to Me void,
but it shall accomplish
what I please,
and it shall prosper
in the thing for which I sent it."

ISAIAH 55:10-11

So then faith comes by hearing, and
hearing by the word of God.

ROMANS 10:17

My son, give attention to my words;
incline your ear to my sayings.
Do not let them depart from your eyes;
keep them in the midst of your heart;
for they are life to those who find them,
and health to all their flesh.

PROVERBS 4:20-22

"If you abide in My word,
you are My disciples indeed.
And you shall know the truth,
and the truth shall make you free."

JOHN 8:31-32

Great peace have those who love Your law,

and nothing causes them to stumble.

PSALM 119:165

21

"This Book of the Law shall
not depart from your mouth,
but you shall meditate in it day and night,
that you may observe to do according
to all that is written in it.
For then you will make your way prosperous,
and then you will have good success."

JOSHUA 1:8

The steps of a good man are ordered
by the LORD, and He delights in his way.
Though he fall, he shall not be utterly cast down;
for the LORD upholds him
with His hand.

PSALM 37:23-24

The counsel of the LORD stands forever,

the plans of His heart to all generations.

PSALM 33:11

As for God, His way is perfect;

the word of the LORD is proven;

He is a shield to all who trust in Him.

PSALM 18:30

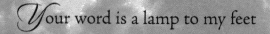

*Y*our word is a lamp to my feet

and a light to my path.

PSALM 119:105

The word of the LORD

endures forever.

1 PETER 1:25

I wait for the LORD, my soul waits,

and in His word I do hope.

PSALM 130:5

"*B*lessed are those who hear

the word of God and keep it!"

LUKE 11:28

*M*an shall not live by bread alone;

but man lives by every word

that proceeds from the mouth

of the LORD.

DEUTERONOMY 8:3

*Y*our word I have hidden in my heart,

that I might not sin against You.

PSALM 119:11

$\mathcal{B}$lessed is he who reads

and those who hear the words

of this prophecy,

and keep those things

which are written in it.

REVELATION 1:3

$\mathcal{I}$ rise before the dawning of the morning,

and cry for help; I hope in Your word.

PSALM 119:147

The righteousness

of Your testimonies is everlasting;

give me understanding,

and I shall live.

PSALM 119:144

"If anyone loves Me,

he will keep My word;

and My Father will love him,

and We will come to him

and make Our home with him."

JOHN 14:23

The Light of Salvation

Thomas
Kinkade

Promises That God Saves from Sin

He could have seen the weeds and gone His way.
After all, who wants a garden filled with worthless garbage?
Wilted, we could only wait for grace.

Then, like the dawn of a new day, mercy arose. Bright as the
sun, Christ's righteousness shined on our hardened hearts and
hope was reborn. No more striving in our own strength. Simply
soak in His light and live—abundantly, prolifically, eternally.

"For God so loved the world

that He gave His only begotten Son,

that whoever believes in Him

should not perish

but have everlasting life."

JOHN 3:16

The Lord is not slack concerning His promise,

as some count slackness,

but is longsuffering toward us,

not willing that any should perish

but that all should come to repentance.

2 PETER 3:9

For the wages of sin is death,

but the gift of God is eternal life

in Christ Jesus our Lord.

ROMANS 6:23

In Him we have redemption through

His blood, the forgiveness of sins,

according to the riches of His grace.

EPHESIANS 1:7

For it is the God who commanded light
to shine out of darkness,
who has shone in our hearts
to give the light of the knowledge
of the glory of God
in the face of Jesus Christ.

2 CORINTHIANS 4:6

Thomas Kinkade

"For the Son of Man has come
to seek and to save that which was lost."

LUKE 19:10

For when we were still without strength,

in due time Christ died for the ungodly.

For scarcely for a righteous man will one die;

yet perhaps for a good man

someone would even dare to die.

But God demonstrates His own love toward us,

in that while we were still sinners,

Christ died for us.

ROMANS 5:6-8

And we know that the Son of God has
come and has given us an understanding,
that we may know Him who is true;
and we are in Him who is true,
in His Son Jesus Christ.
This is the true God and eternal life.

1 JOHN 5:20

For I delivered to you first of all
that which I also received:
that Christ died for our sins
according to the Scriptures.

1 CORINTHIANS 15:3

"For God did not send His Son into the world

to condemn the world,

but that the world through Him

might be saved."

JOHN 3:17

"*A*nd she will bring forth a Son,

and you shall call His name Jesus,

for He will save His people

from their sins."

MATTHEW 1:21

*W*ho has saved us and called us

with a holy calling,

not according to our works,

but according to His own purpose and grace

which was given to us in Christ Jesus

before time began.

2 TIMOTHY 1:9

So they said,
"Believe on the Lord Jesus Christ,
and you will be saved,
you and your household."

ACTS 16:31

That if you confess
with your mouth the Lord Jesus
and believe in your heart
that God has raised Him from the dead,
you will be saved.
For with the heart
one believes unto righteousness,
and with the mouth confession
is made unto salvation.

ROMANS 10:9-10

For by grace you have been saved through faith,

and that not of yourselves;

it is the gift of God.

EPHESIANS 2:8

For "whoever calls
on the name of the LORD
shall be saved."

ROMANS 10:13

I will greatly rejoice in the LORD,
my soul shall be joyful in my God;
for He has clothed me
with the garments of salvation,
He has covered me
with the robe of righteousness,
as a bridegroom decks himself
with ornaments,
and as a bride adorns herself
with her jewels.

ISAIAH 61:10

Therefore, having been

justified by faith,

we have peace with God

through our Lord Jesus Christ.

ROMANS 5:1

"For I will be merciful

to their unrighteousness,

and their sins and their lawless deeds

I will remember no more."

HEBREWS 8:12

"Come now, and let us reason together,"
says the LORD, "though your sins are like scarlet,
they shall be as white as snow;
though they are red like crimson,
they shall be as wool."

ISAIAH 1:18

Thomas
Kinkade

There is therefore now no condemnation
to those who are in Christ Jesus,
who do not walk according to the flesh,
but according to the Spirit.

ROMANS 8:1

Knowing that a man is not justified
by the works of the law
but by faith in Jesus Christ,
even we have believed in Christ Jesus,
that we might be justified
by faith in Christ.

GALATIANS 2:16

For I am not ashamed
of the gospel of Christ,
for it is the power of God to salvation
for everyone who believes,
for the Jew first and also for the Greek.

ROMANS 1:16

For the grace of God
that brings salvation
has appeared to all men,
teaching us that,
denying ungodliness and worldly lusts,
we should live soberly, righteously,
and godly in the present age.

TITUS 2:11-12

The Light of Hope

to do list...

Promises for Spiritual Growth

*True art is a process. It is gentle pigments working in
harmony until slowly, with time tempering the strokes,
a transition takes place. White canvas is washed with color.
And an ideal world of life enthralls the ones who come to watch.*

*Our walk with Christ is much the same. Every moment
surrendered to the Lord's leadership becomes a stroke of His life
painted into us. And others will watch in wonder as Christ's
portrait unfolds and radiates the brilliant colors of
Christ's hope and joy in us.*

Thomas Kinkade

For we walk by faith,

not by sight.

2 CORINTHIANS 5:7

That the genuineness of your faith,

being much more precious

than gold that perishes,

though it is tested by fire,

may be found to praise,

honor, and glory

at the revelation of Jesus Christ.

1 PETER 1:7

But the Lord is faithful,

who will establish you

and guard you

from the evil one.

2 THESSALONIANS 3:3

Blessed is the man

who endures temptation;

for when he has been approved,

he will receive the crown of life

which the Lord has promised

to those who love Him.

JAMES 1:12

"I am the vine, you are the branches.
He who abides in Me, and I in him,
bears much fruit;
for without Me you can do nothing."

JOHN 15:5

"For the eyes of the LORD
run to and fro
throughout the whole earth,
to show Himself strong
on behalf of those whose heart
is loyal to Him."

2 CHRONICLES 16:9

"He who has My commandments
and keeps them,
it is he who loves Me.
And he who loves Me
will be loved by My Father,
and I will love him
and manifest Myself to him."

JOHN 14:21

*B*ut as it is written:

"Eye has not seen, nor ear heard,

nor have entered into the heart of man

the things which God has prepared

for those who love Him."

1 CORINTHIANS 2:9

"*A*nd you shall love the LORD your God

with all your heart, with all your soul,

with all your mind, and with all your strength."

This is the first commandment.

MARK 12:30

And we know

that all things work together for good

to those who love God,

to those who are the called

according to His purpose.

ROMANS 8:28

$\mathcal{B}$e anxious for nothing,
but in everything
by prayer and supplication,
with thanksgiving,
let your requests be made known to God;
and the peace of God,
which surpasses all understanding,
will guard your hearts and minds
through Christ Jesus.

PHILIPPIANS 4:6-7

"$\mathcal{P}$eace I leave with you,
My peace I give to you;
not as the world gives do I give to you.
Let not your heart be troubled,
neither let it be afraid."

JOHN 14:27

If any of you lacks wisdom,
let him ask of God,
who gives to all liberally and without reproach,
and it will be given to him.

JAMES 1:5

If you seek her as silver,
and search for her as for hidden treasures;
then you will understand the fear of the LORD,
and find the knowledge of God.
For the LORD gives wisdom;
from His mouth
come knowledge and understanding;
He stores up sound wisdom for the upright;
He is a shield to those who walk uprightly.

PROVERBS 2:4-7

*W*hen you pass through the waters,
I will be with you; and through the rivers,
they shall not overflow you.
When you walk through the fire,
you shall not be burned,
nor shall the flame scorch you.

ISAIAH 43:2

Thomas Kinkade

*N*ow may the God of hope

fill you with all joy and peace in believing,

that you may abound in hope

by the power of the Holy Spirit.

ROMANS 15:13

*B*eing confident of this very thing,

that He who has begun a good work in you

will complete it

until the day of Jesus Christ.

PHILIPPIANS 1:6

The fear of the LORD
is the beginning of wisdom;
a good understanding have all those
who do His commandments.

PSALM 111:10

"A new commandment I give to you,
that you love one another;
as I have loved you,
that you also love one another.
By this all will know
that you are My disciples,
if you have love for one another."

JOHN 13:34-35

Finally, my brethren, be strong in the Lord
and in the power of His might.
Put on the whole armor of God,
that you may be able to stand against
the wiles of the devil.

EPHESIANS 6:10-11

Thomas Kinkade

*A*nd if Christ is in you,
the body is dead because of sin,
but the Spirit is life
because of righteousness.

ROMANS 8:10

"*T*hen I will give them one heart,
and I will put a new spirit within them,
and take the stony heart out of their flesh,
and give them a heart of flesh,
that they may walk in My statutes
and keep My judgments and do them;
and they shall be My people,
and I will be their God."

EZEKIEL 11:19-20

$\mathcal{B}$ecome complete. Be of good comfort,

be of one mind, live in peace;

and the God of love and peace

will be with you.

2 CORINTHIANS 13:11

$\mathcal{N}$ow may the God of peace Himself

sanctify you completely;

and may your whole spirit, soul, and body

be preserved blameless

at the coming of our Lord Jesus Christ.

1 THESSALONIANS 5:23

Strength Renewed

Promises for Your Personal Needs, Family, and Relationships

As a child, I used to wish away the rain. Summer storms
supplanted outdoor adventures, so I relished instead
the droughts that kept my days dry.

As an adult, I find that old habits die hard. I still secretly
hope to sail through life unscathed by storms that would otherwise
strengthen my faith. But God knows I need the rain to grow.
My strength lies behind the dark skies where His light still
shines—and sends out rays at just the right time,
turning the rain into brilliant rainbows.

God is our refuge and strength,

a very present help in trouble.

Therefore we will not fear,

even though the earth be removed,

and though the mountains be carried

into the midst of the sea;

though its waters roar and be troubled,

though the mountains shake with its swelling.

PSALM 46:1-3

It is good that one should hope

and wait quietly

for the salvation of the LORD.

LAMENTATIONS 3:26

We are hard-pressed on every side,

yet not crushed;

we are perplexed, but not in despair;

persecuted, but not forsaken;

struck down, but not destroyed.

2 CORINTHIANS 4:8-9

*B*ehold, the eye of the LORD

is on those who fear Him,

on those who hope in His mercy.

PSALM 33:18

"*Let* your light so shine before men,

that they may see your good works

and glorify your Father in heaven."

MATTHEW 5:16

The salvation of the righteous
is from the LORD;
He is their strength
in the time of trouble.

PSALM 37:39

Blessed is every one who fears the LORD,
who walks in His ways.
When you eat the labor of your hands,
you shall be happy,
and it shall be well with you.
Your wife shall be like a fruitful vine
in the very heart of your house,
your children like olive plants
all around your table.
Behold, thus shall the man be blessed
who fears the LORD.

PSALM 128:1-4

Though I walk in the midst of trouble,

You will revive me;

You will stretch out Your hand

against the wrath of my enemies,

and Your right hand

will save me.

PSALM 138:7

He shall regard the prayer of the destitute,

and shall not despise their prayer.

PSALM 102:17

Through wisdom a house is built,

and by understanding

it is established.

PROVERBS 24:3

The LORD is good,

a stronghold in the day of trouble;

and He knows those

who trust in Him.

NAHUM 1:7

My brethren, count it all joy

when you fall into various trials,

knowing that the testing of your faith

produces patience.

JAMES 1:2-3

Behold,
children are a heritage from the LORD,
the fruit of the womb is a reward.
Like arrows in the hand of a warrior,
so are the children of one's youth.
Happy is the man
who has his quiver full of them;
they shall not be ashamed,
but shall speak with their enemies in the gate.

PSALM 127:3-5

All your children
shall be taught by the LORD,
and great shall be
the peace of your children.

ISAIAH 54:13

$\mathcal{Y}$ou are my hiding place;
You shall preserve me from trouble;
You shall surround me with songs of deliverance.

PSALM 32:7

"*Be* strong and of good courage,
do not fear nor be afraid of them;
for the LORD your God,
He is the One who goes with you.
He will not leave you nor forsake you."

DEUTERONOMY 31:6

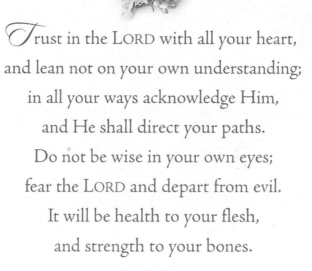

*T*rust in the LORD with all your heart,
and lean not on your own understanding;
in all your ways acknowledge Him,
and He shall direct your paths.
Do not be wise in your own eyes;
fear the LORD and depart from evil.
It will be health to your flesh,
and strength to your bones.

PROVERBS 3:5-8

"The LORD will command the blessing
on you in your storehouses
and in all to which you set your hand,
and He will bless you in the land
which the LORD your God is giving you."

DEUTERONOMY 28:8

"A new commandment I give to you,
that you love one another;
as I have loved you,
that you also love one another.
By this all will know
that you are My disciples,
if you have love for one another."

JOHN 13:34-35

Surely goodness and mercy

shall follow me all the days of my life;

and I will dwell in the house of the LORD forever.

PSALM 23:6

*N*ow may the God of patience and comfort
grant you to be like-minded
toward one another,
according to Christ Jesus,
that you may with one mind
and one mouth
glorify the God and Father
of our Lord Jesus Christ.

ROMANS 15:5-6

*E*ven to your old age, I am He,
and even to gray hairs I will carry you!
I have made, and I will bear;
even I will carry, and will deliver you.

ISAIAH 46:4

*L*et no corrupt word proceed

out of your mouth,

but what is good for necessary edification,

that it may impart grace

to the hearers.

EPHESIANS 4:29

*L*et your conduct be without covetousness;

be content with such things as you have.

For He Himself has said,

"I will never leave you nor forsake you."

HEBREWS 13:5

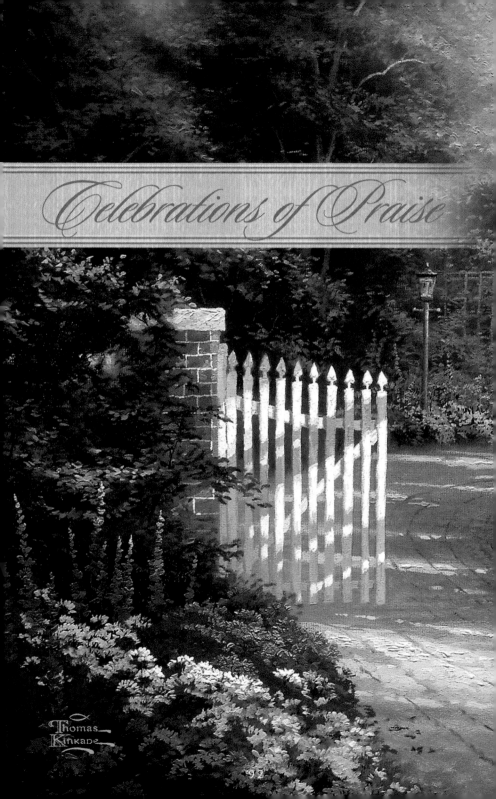

Celebrations of Praise

Promises of the Triumph of Righteousness, and Psalms of Worship and Praise

Springtime blooms celebrate the news. Summer answers with its own steady strength. Fall follows with an amber encore, and winter washes the palette clean with a world whitened by snow.

They are different seasons, each with their own reasons to sing their Creator's praise. And our lives are the same. Though some times may seem easier than others, every season of our souls harbors seeds of hope that can spring forth in celebration. Life's moments simply must be sown in the light of His love— then we can't help but see God's beauty our whole life long.

I will sing of the mercies
of the LORD forever;
with my mouth will I make known
Your faithfulness to all generations.

PSALM 89:1

"*F*ear not, for I am with you;
be not dismayed,
for I am your God.
I will strengthen you,
yes, I will help you,
I will uphold you
with My righteous right hand."

ISAIAH 41:10

"*I*, the LORD,
have called You in righteousness,
and will hold Your hand;
I will keep You and give You
as a covenant to the people,
as a light to the Gentiles."

ISAIAH 42:6

*H*ow beautiful upon the mountains
are the feet of him
who brings good news,
who proclaims peace,
who brings glad tidings of good things,
who proclaims salvation,
who says to Zion,
"Your God reigns!"

ISAIAH 52:7

" *The* sun shall no longer be your light by day,

nor for brightness shall the moon give light to you;

but the LORD will be to you an everlasting light,

and your God your glory."

ISAIAH 60:19

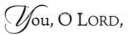

You, O LORD,
are a shield for me,
my glory and the One
who lifts up my head.

PSALM 3:3

The wolf also shall dwell with the lamb,
the leopard shall lie down with the young goat,
the calf and the young lion
and the fatling together;
and a little child shall lead them. . . .
They shall not hurt nor destroy
in all My holy mountain,
for the earth shall be full of the knowledge
of the LORD as the waters cover the sea."

ISAIAH 11:6, 9

"Also your people shall all be righteous;
they shall inherit the land forever,
the branch of My planting,
the work of My hands,
that I may be glorified."

ISAIAH 60:21

Let all those rejoice
who put their trust in You;
let them ever shout for joy,
because You defend them;
let those also who love Your name
be joyful in You.
For You, O LORD, will bless the righteous;
with favor You will surround him
as with a shield.

PSALM 5:11-12

You will show me the path of life;

in Your presence is fullness of joy;

at Your right hand

are pleasures forevermore.

PSALM 16:11

I will praise You, O LORD,

with my whole heart;

I will tell of all Your marvelous works.

I will be glad and rejoice in You;

I will sing praise to Your name,

O Most High.

PSALM 9:1-2

*B*ut I have trusted in Your mercy;

my heart shall rejoice in Your salvation.

I will sing to the LORD,

because He has dealt bountifully with me.

PSALM 13:5-6

All the ends of the world
shall remember and turn to the LORD,
and all the families of the nations
shall worship before You.
For the kingdom is the LORD's,
and He rules over the nations.

PSALM 22:27-28

Oh, send out Your light and Your truth!
Let them lead me;
let them bring me to Your holy hill
and to Your tabernacle.
Then I will go to the altar of God,
to God my exceeding joy;
and on the harp I will praise You,
O God, my God.

PSALM 43:3-4

$\mathcal{T}$hose who are wise shall shine

like the brightness of the firmament,

and those who turn many to righteousness

like the stars forever and ever.

DANIEL 12:3

Thomas
Kinkade

The righteous shall be glad in the LORD,

and trust in Him.

And all the upright in heart shall glory.

PSALM 64:10

Because Your lovingkindness

is better than life,

my lips shall praise You.

Thus I will bless You while I live;

I will lift up my hands in Your name.

PSALM 63:3-4

Make a joyful shout to God,

all the earth!

Sing out the honor of His name;

make His praise glorious. . . .

"All the earth shall worship You

and sing praises to You;

they shall sing praises to Your name."

PSALM 66:1-2, 4

Blessed be God,

who has not turned away my prayer,

nor His mercy from me!

PSALM 66:20

Your mercy, O LORD, is in the heavens;
Your faithfulness reaches to the clouds.
Your righteousness is like the great mountains;
Your judgments are a great deep;
O LORD, You preserve man and beast.

PSALM 36:5-6

$\mathcal{I}$ will hope continually,

and will praise You yet more and more.

My mouth shall tell of Your righteousness

and Your salvation all the day,

for I do not know their limits.

PSALM 71:14-15

$\mathcal{B}$lessed be the LORD God,

the God of Israel,

who only does wondrous things!

And blessed be His glorious name forever!

And let the whole earth

be filled with His glory.

Amen and Amen.

PSALM 72:18-19

*S*ing praise to the LORD,

you saints of His,

and give thanks

at the remembrance

of His holy name.

PSALM 30:4

O LORD, our Lord,

how excellent is Your name

in all the earth,

who have set Your glory

above the heavens!

PSALM 8:1

Special Thoughts & Memories